Poems from the heart

I wear a mask

No not because of covid

I wear a mask, like others do

To hide

To pretend not to be me

Me

Who is that?

I've worn a mask so long

And changed my mask so often

I no longer know

Do you?

We all wear the mask

Do we ever really take it off?

Or just change it?

One mask for home

One mask for work

Another mask for friends and family

A different one for strangers and those we just met

They say we take off our masks for those we love

And those that love us

But do we?

Do any of us truly exist?
Or our we just an accumulation of the masks we wear?

The old cat

The old cat moved slowly
He so badly wanted the warm embrace of a loving human
But… he had been rejected, chased and hurt so many times
He was afraid

The old man moved slowly
He so badly wanted the warm touch of a loving presence
But he had been rejected, chased and hurt so many times
He was afraid.

The old cat moved closer
The old man did not yell or chase him
The old man slowly put out his hand
The old cat did not run from him

The old cat sniffed the hand
The old man softly and slowly touched his head
The old cat began to purr
It had been so long since he had felt a gentle touch

The old cat rubbed up against the old man
The old man smiled and let out a joyful sigh
The old cat climbed into the man's lap
The old man gently stroked every part of the cat

The old cat hoped he had found his person
The old man hoped he had found his loving presence
The old man said aloud"I will give you I home if you'll have me"
The old cat gratefully accepted

And thus the old cat and the old man found each other
And in so doing they each found the love, warmth and acceptance they were looking for

Eyes

My dogs eyes show me love

My cat's eyes show me gratitude

Human eyes show me demands

My own eyes show me despair

Gods eyes show me hope

School Shooting

Guns shoot

People die

Why?

Love Fails

Hatred Reigns

Caine?

Good Gone

Evil Wins

Sins?

Need faith

Do not despair

Care

Caregivers Lament

Feet up

Time to Relax

Okay

Naaaaaaaaan!

Yard work

Start to cook

Me time

Naaaaaan!

Cleaning

Now dressing him

Rest now

Naaaaaaaan!

No end

What about me?

My turn?

Naaaaaaaa!

For Mom

You provided :

Understanding

Comfort

Safety

For that we are grateful

You taught us;

Compassion

Persistance

Self-reliance

For that we are grateful

You showed us the importance of:

Family

Friends

Pets

For that we are grateful
I

You gave us:

Hope

Faith

Wisdom

For that we are grateful

You fought for us and with us

For that we are grateful

You stood:

With us

Behind us to push us

And before us to defend us

For that we are grateful

We give you our:

Admiration

Gratitude and

LOVE

To a Lovely Young Lady

There is nothing as wonderful as a baby girl,

All peaches and cream sleeping in her crib

No there's nothing as wonderful as a baby girl

Unless-unless its a toddler

A tiny, wee, lass waddling from side to side like

A little duck

Diaper plumped out, ruffled rubber panties peaking out

From under her frilly little dress

No there's nothing as wonderful as a little toddler

Unless-unless- it's a little pre-school girl

Emptying out the refrigerator, mixing up a delightful

Batch of soap flakes, cleanser, eggs and sugar.

"I was making a surprise for you mommy".

Going through your good make up, blue eye shadow

On her nose, lipstick on her checks , and your good

Alligator pumps on her fee.

No there's nothing as wonderful as a pre-school girl

Unless-unless- its a seven, eight or nine year old

Leaving for school each morning all scrubbed and shinny.

Coming home yelling"mama, can you bake a cake for me. I need it by seven o'clock tonight.

promised the P.T.A. and forgot to tell you. Aw,ma, I promised."

No there is nothing as wonderful as a seven, eight or nine year old

Unless-unless- it 's a pre-teener.

"Ma,ma,why don't I have a bust. Everyone in my class does. Can I buy a padded bra?

"Everyone's wearing padded bras. Why an't I wear make-up to school?
I bought it with my own money."

No there's nothing as exciting or wonderful as a pre-teener

Unless-unless- it's a teen age girl.

A teen age girl is idealistic, down to earth, flighty, dependable, shy, outgoing.

A teen age girl is a human kaleidoscope.

And with it all, a mind developing, so razor keen it can cut through your

Arguments and theories, like a skilled surgeon with a sharp scalpel

One day after a rousing family discussion , your husband and you will look at each

Other in

Amazement and silently ask "when did this happen?"

No there's nothing as wonderful as a teen age girl.

Unless-unless- it's a lovely young lady.

One who is considerate, compassionate, who is self-assured, who knows who she is

And where she is going.

No there's nothing as wonderful as a lovely young lady, when she is a very special

Young lady,

Your very own daughter

To Nancy (on her 16th birthday)

There comes a time in every girl's life

When she's no longer a child

And she's too young for a wife

These are known as the golden years

Your growth is nurtured by joy and by tears

Learn and grow and use these years well

For they will determine if life's heaven or hell

I wish I could lead you or show you the way

But you are the one that must choose day by day

An so my darling, my angel, my star

All I can do is watch from afar

I know that you will stumble and trip on the way

And all any mother can do is to pray

I hope that the joy you have given to others

Will come back to you from your "Sisters and brothers"

I pray that your friendship so loyal and true

Will double and triple and come back to you

I wish that your reverence for all kinds of life

Would encircle the earth, and thus end its strife

And yet my darling, my angel, my star,

All I can do is watch from afar

For my Son (Son)

You were my hopes and my dreams

The protector and the protected

My day started and ended with your love

As yours did with mine

It was the constant in my life

As mine was the constant in yours

I made mistakes

You never saw them

You had your faults

But not in my eyes

 I helped you grow

You helped me more

Your Father came for you

I cried and let you go

Trust in God

Where are we going mommy

Where are we going?

I don't know my darling

I don't know

Where is my Daddy, Mommy?

Where is my Daddy?

I don't know my darling.

I don't know

Will we be safe Mommy?

Will we be safe?

Trust in God my darling.

Trust in God.

Contentment

I am not hungry

I am not thirsty

I am not hot

I am not cold

My bed is soft and warm

I am safe

I am loved

I am ….. content

The Dogs of my Life

Mischief maker

Joy of life

Protecter

My love, my life

Sandpaper thief,

Daddy's girl

Her life's creed

Adapt, adapt

True gentleman

Always good

Kindest heart

Gentle giant

Mommy's baby

Spoiled most

Sharing love

Always playful

Most grateful girl

6 months waiting

Till mommy came

She knew at once

No time to spare

Time is passing

Too quickly

I'm feeling old

Leaves turning

Wrong choices made

Or were they?

Is there still time

To be me?

The empty box

Many memories I've held

Many journeys I have traveled

Four corners

East, west, north, south

I've seen it all

Both good and bad

Always interesting

Now I'm old and tattered

My seams are bursting

Ready to be recycled

                    Quiet

Alone

Me and my thoughts

Heavenly

Desolate

Emptiness

Missing my animals

Nobody else

Dreaming

Me time

Alone, not lonely

Supported by Faith

Dawn

The day starts

The sun is climbing in the sky

Rising, rising

It reaches its zenith

Calm, peaceful, quiet

A burst of color

Sunset

Glorious colors

Purple and gold and red

And then its gone

Evening

The sun has disappeared

Twinkling stars

Magnificent moon arises

High in the sky

And then

It is overtaken by the sun

The Feral/Stray Cat's Thanksgiving Prayer

I am thankful for my

Steady food supply

I am grateful for my

Safe, warm place to sleep

I appreciate the people

Who don't chase me but

Talk softly to me and give me a loving touch

Dear Lord please bless

Those that care for me

And about me

Amen

Blindsided

I never saw the signals

I ignored all of the signs

My friends showed me the red flags

My family stood by my side

I was totally blindsided

I really shouldn't have been

The warnings were all over

My blindness was my own

Now I look back on the years

I see what others saw

A ask myself,"what now?

What does my future hold"?

Don't forget the past

But don't Dwell on it

Learn from your mistakes

Find your passions and embrace them

                          Give me a chance

Look into my eyes

See the love that's waiting

Give me a chance

I will give you my heart

I will be your loyal friend

You will be my sun, moon and stars

Unlike a human

I will never betray you

I will never forsake you

My love will be unconditional

Give me a chance

The Feral/stray Cat's thanksgiving Prayer

I am thankful for my steady food supply

I am grateful for my

Safe, warm place to sleep

I appreciate the people

Who don't chase me but

Talk softly to me and give me a loving touch

Dear Lord please bless

Those that care for me

And about me

Amen

The Stray Cat's Wish

Safe in her shelter

She happily sleeps

Her belly is full

She knows she is loved

She happily sleeps

No danger to fear

Gentle hands pet her

She knows she is loved

No danger will get her

She's safe and she's warm

She knows she is loved

She still wants a home

No danger will get her

She'll never lack food

She still wants a home

Safe in her shelter

Holiday Memories

The presents are wrapped

The cooking is done

The candles are lit

The decorations finished

The cooking is done

Now cleanup is needed

The decorations finished

Now to be put away

Now clean up is needed

Memories to be relieved

Now to be put away

To be saved forever

Memories to be relieved

Hope for the future

Now to be put away

The presents are wrapped

Made in the USA
Middletown, DE
28 July 2024

58026834R00015